Financial Reporting International Standards

CIMA PUBLISHING

ELSEVIER

AMSTERDAM . BOSTON . HEIDELBERG . LONDON . NEW YORK . OXFORD
PARIS . SAN DIEGO . SAN FRANCISCO . SINGAPORE . SYDNEY . TOKYO

CIMA Publishing
An imprint of Elsevier
Linacre House, Jordan Hill, Oxford OX2 8DP
200 Wheeler Road, Burlington MA 01803

First published 2004

British Library Cataloguing in Publication Data
A catalogue record for this book is available from the British Library

ISBN 0 7506 6237 9

For information of all CIMA publications
visit our website at www.cimapublishing.com

Transferred to Digital Printing 2009

CIMA

November 2003 Examinations

Intermediate Level

Financial Reporting – International Standards
(IFRI – Paper 7b)

The answers published here have been written by the Examiner and should provide a helpful guide for both lecturers and students.

Published separately on the CIMA website (www.cimaglobal.com/students) from the end of March 2004 is a Post Examination Guide for this paper, which provides much valuable and complementary material including indicative mark information.

CIMA

Intermediate Level

Financial Reporting – International Accounting Standards

7b

IFRI

19 November 2003

Wednesday morning

INSTRUCTIONS TO CANDIDATES

Read this page before you look at the questions

You are allowed three hours to answer this question paper.
This question paper is based on INTERNATIONAL ACCOUNTING STANDARDS. If you require the paper based on UK Accounting Standards, please speak immediately to the invigilator.
Answer the ONE question in section A (this has 10 sub-questions). Answer the ONE question in section B. Answer TWO questions only from section C.
Maths Tables and Formulae are provided on pages 17 – 19.
Write your examination number, your contact ID and your name on a double-sided card, which must be attached to your answer book. Write IFRI on the line marked "Subject" on the front of the answer book.
Do NOT write your name or your contact ID anywhere on this booklet.
Tick the appropriate boxes on the front of the answer book to indicate which questions you have answered.

SECTION A — 20 MARKS

ANSWER *ALL* TEN SUB-QUESTIONS

Each of the sub-questions numbered from **1.1** to **1.10** inclusive, given below, has only ONE correct answer.

REQUIRED:
On the SPECIAL ANSWER SHEET opposite, place a circle "O" around the letter that gives the correct answer to each sub-question.

If you wish to change your mind about an answer, block out your first answer completely and then circle another letter. You will NOT receive marks if more than one letter is circled.

Please note that you will NOT receive marks for any workings to these sub-questions.

You must detach the special answer sheet from the question paper and attach it to the inside front cover of your answer book before you hand it to the invigilators at the end of the examination.

Question One

1.1 Parent owns 80% of the equity share capital of Child, its only subsidiary. The following information is extracted from the individual balance sheets of the two companies on 30 September 2003:

	Parent	*Child*
	$	*$*
Current assets	600,000	450,000
Current liabilities	350,000	300,000

The current liabilities of Child include $80,000 in respect of a dividend that was declared before 30 September 2003 and paid on 31 October 2003. Parent recognises investment income on a cash basis.

If there are no other intra-group balances, what is the value of the consolidated net current assets (current assets less current liabilities) of Parent at 30 September 2003.

A $320,000

B $400,000

C $464,000

D $400,000

1.2 Foot owns 150,000 of the issued ordinary shares and 60,000 of the issued preferred shares of Step (its only subsidiary). The balance sheets of the two enterprises at 31 August 2003 showed the following:

	Foot	*Step*
	$000	*$000*
Ordinary shares of $1	500	250
Preferred shares of $1	100	150
Accumulated profits	250	170
	850	570

What is the minority interest that will appear in the consolidated balance sheet of Foot at 31 August 2003?

A $228,000

B $258,000

C $292,000

D $342,000

1.3 On 30 June 2003, Sugar entered into an agreement with two other investors to establish a new enterprise, Spice. All three investors subscribed for $^1/_3$ of the equity shares in Spice and each share carries one vote. All three investors appointed two representatives to the six-member board of directors of Spice. All key policy decisions require the agreement of five of the six board members.

The following statements refer to the treatment of the investment in Spice in the consolidated financial statements of Sugar for the year ended 30 September 2003:

(i) Spice will be treated as a joint venture simply because the three investors hold $^1/_3$ of the shares each.

(ii) Spice will be treated as a joint venture in this case, but only because of the requirement that key policy decisions require the consent of at least five of the directors.

(iii) If Spice carries on a business that is distinct from that of its investors, then it will be consolidated using proportional consolidation.

(iv) Spice is only a joint venture if the requirement that key policy decisions require the consent of five directors is established by contract.

Assuming the benchmark treatment set out in IAS 31 – *Financial Reporting of Interests in Joint Ventures* – is used, which of the above statements are true?

A (i) and (iii) only.

B (i), (iii) and (iv) only.

C (ii) and (iii) only.

D (ii), (iii) and (iv) only.

1.4 On 1 July 1994, Super acquired 75% of the ordinary shares in Man for $6 million. Goodwill on consolidation of $1 million was amortised on a monthly basis over 20 years or 240 months).

On 31 December 2002 (102 months after acquisition), Super disposed of part of its shareholding in Man for $4 million, retaining a 40% interest. The net assets of Man on 1 July 2002 were $8·5 million and Man made a profit of $800,000 in the year ended 30 June 2003 (no dividends were paid or declared by Man in that year).

What is the profit on disposal that will be included in the consolidated income statement of Super for the year ended 30 June 2003?

A $616,667

B $683,750

C $885,000

D $1,200,000

1.5 Near has a subsidiary, Faraway, that prepares its financial statements in florins. Near owns 80% of the ordinary shares of Faraway.

On 1 October 2002, the net assets of Faraway that were included in the consolidated balance sheet of Near had a carrying value of 40 million florins. The profit of Faraway for the year ended 30 September 2003 was 4·5 million florins. Near translates the financial statements of Faraway for consolidation purposes using the closing rate method.

Relevant exchange rates are as follows:

Date	*Exchange rate [florins to $1]*
1 October 2002	2·5
30 September 2003	2·0
Average for the year ended 30 September 2003	2·25

Ignoring goodwill on consolidation, what is the exchange gain relating to Faraway that will be taken to the consolidated statement of changes in equity of Near for the year ended 30 September 2003?

A $3,200,000

B $3,400,000

C $4,000,000

D $4,250,000

1.6 A cash-generating unit was reviewed for impairment at 31 May 2003 as required by IAS 36 – *Impairment of assets*. The impairment review revealed that the cash-generating unit had a value in use of $25 million and a net realisable value of $23 million.

The carrying values of the net assets of the cash-generating unit immediately prior to the impairment review were as follows:

	$000
Goodwill	5,000
Property, plant and equipment	18,000
Net current assets	4,000
	27,000

The review indicated that an item of plant (included in the above figure of $18 million) with a carrying value of $1 million had been severely damaged and was virtually worthless. There was no other evidence of obvious impairment to specific assets.

What is the carrying value of the goodwill relating to the unit immediately after the results of the impairment review have been reflected in accordance with IAS 36?

A $1 million

B $2 million

C $3 million

D $4 million

1.7 Spencer has produced draft consolidated financial statements for the year ended 30 June 2003. These financial statements include a deferred tax liability of $8 million. However, no account has been taken of the potential deferred tax implications of the following:

(i) On 30 June 2003, the group revalued all its properties and a surplus of $7 million was taken to the statement of changes in equity. The group has no intention of disposing of any of these properties in the foreseeable future.

(ii) One of the subsidiaries of Spencer made a loss adjusted for tax purposes of $2 million in the year ended 30 June 2003. This loss can only be relieved against future trading profits made by the subsidiary. The directors of Spencer believe the loss made by the subsidiary to be attributable to non-recurring factors.

What is the deferred tax liability of Spencer at 30 June 2003 under the provisions of IAS 12 – *Income Taxes* after taking account of both the above events? [Use a rate of tax of 30% where required.]

A $7·4 million

B $8 million

C $9·5 million

D $10·1 million

1.8 B issued new interest-bearing borrowings to finance a construction project on the following terms:

- The new borrowings had a nominal value of $50 million.
- The borrowings carried an annual interest rate of 4%.
- The costs of issuing the borrowings totalled $600,000. This comprised underwriting fees relating to the issue of $500,000 and fees of $100,000 payable for general advice on which of a number of sources of finance should be pursued.
- The borrowings were theoretically repayable at $60 million after five years. However, the borrowings contained an option to convert into ordinary shares after five years as an alternative to repayment. At the date of issue, the directors of B were virtually certain that the investors would choose the conversion option.

What is the total financing cost relating to these borrowings?

A $10·5 million

B $10·6 million

C $20·5 million

D $20·6 million

1.9 The following statements relate to accounting for retirement benefits under the provisions of IAS 19 – *Employee benefits.* [The "net pension asset" is the fair value of plan assets less the present value of plan liabilities.]

(i) Other things being equal, the net pension asset increases when interest rates increase.

(ii) Other things being equal, the net pension asset decreases when share prices fall.

(iii) Where the terms of retirement benefits are altered so as to provide immediate additional benefits to retired members, then the cost of the additional benefits should be recognised in the income statement over a period equal to the average life expectancy of the retired members.

Which of the statements are true?

A (i) and (ii) only.

B (i) and (iii) only.

C (ii) and (iii) only.

D All of them.

1.10 Experimenter appraises projects using a cost of capital of 12%. All non-current assets of Experimenter are depreciated on a straight-line basis over their useful economic lives.

On 1 July 2002, Experimenter opened a chemical reprocessing plant. The plant was due to be active for five years until 30 June 2007, when it would be decommissioned. At 1 July 2002, the costs of decommissioning the plant were estimated to be $4 million.

What is the total charge to the income statement in respect of the decommissioning for the year ended 30 June 2003?

A $453,600

B $725,760

C $800,000

D $2,268,000

(Total = 20 marks)

End of section A

SECTION B – 30 MARKS

ANSWER THIS QUESTION [THE REQUIREMENT IS ON PAGE 13]

Question Two

The balance sheets of George and its subsidiary enterprises Zippy and Bungle at 30 June 2003 (the accounting date for all three enterprises) are given below:

	George		*Zippy*		*Bungle*	
	$000	*$000*	*$000*	*$000*	*$000*	*$000*
ASSETS						
Non-current assets:						
Property, plant and equipment (*Note 3*)	45,000		25,000		20,000	
Financial assets (*Notes 1* and *2*)	20,000		Nil		Nil	
		65,000		25,000		20,000
Current assets:						
Inventories (*Notes 3* and *4*)	18,000		12,000		11,000	
Trade and other receivables (*Notes 3* and *4*)	15,000		10,000		9,000	
		33,000		22,000		20,000
Total assets		98,000		47,000		40,000
EQUITY AND LIABILITIES						
Capital and reserves:						
Issued ordinary share capital ($1 shares)	25,000		15,000		10,000	
10% $1 preferred shares	Nil		10,000		Nil	
Share premium account	10,000		Nil		4,000	
Accumulated profits	24,000		8,000		9,300	
		59,000		33,000		23,300
Non-current liabilities						
Interest bearing borrowing (*Note 3*)	20,000		Nil		4,000	
Deferred tax (*Note 3*)	2,000		1,000		1,500	
		22,000		1,000		5,500
Current liabilities						
Trade payables (*Note 4*)	10,000		6,500		6,000	
Tax payable	2,000		1,500		1,000	
Proposed dividend (*Note 5*)	Nil		1,000		Nil	
Bank overdraft	5,000		4,000		3,000	
Provisions (*Note 3*)	Nil		Nil		1,200	
		17,000		13,000		11,200
Total equity and liabilities		98,000		47,000		40,000

Notes to the balance sheets

1 On 1 July 1990, the date of incorporation of Zippy, George subscribed for all the ordinary shares of Zippy at par. Then, on 1 July 1995, when its balance of accumulated profits was $3 million, Zippy issued 10 million $1 preferred shares at par. George subscribed for 50% of these shares.

2 On 30 June 2003, George purchased 8 million $1 shares in Bungle. The terms of the purchase consideration were as follows:

2.1 On 30 June 2003, George issued 3 $1 ordinary shares for every 4 shares purchased in Bungle. The market value of the ordinary shares at 30 June 2003 was $4 per share.

2.2 On 30 June 2005, George will pay the former shareholders of Bungle $1 in cash for every share in Bungle they have purchased. This payment is contingent on the cumulative profits after tax of Bungle for the two years ending 30 June 2005 being at least $3 million.

At the date of carrying out the fair value exercise (see *Note 3* below), the directors of George considered it probable that this cash payment would be made.

2.3 No entries in respect of the purchase of shares in Bungle have been made in the balance sheet of George that appears on page 10.

3. Following the acquisition of Bungle, the directors of George carried out a fair value exercise as required by IAS 22 – *Business combinations*. The following matters are relevant and all potential fair value adjustments are material:

3.1 Property, plant and equipment comprise land and buildings and plant and machinery. At 30 June 2003, the land and buildings had a carrying value of $12 million and a market value of $18 million. The plant and machinery had a carrying value of $8 million. All the plant and machinery was purchased on 30 June 2000 and was being depreciated on a straight-line basis over 8 years. No reliable estimate was available of the current market value of the plant and machinery, but at 30 June 2003, the plant would have cost $22 million to replace with new plant.

3.2 The inventory at 30 June 2003 comprised:

- Finished goods which could be sold for $14·5 million. A reasonable profit allowance for the selling effort of the group would be $3 million.
- Finished goods that had been damaged and could only be sold for $100,000, representing a significant loss on sale.

3.3 Trade receivables includes an amount of $400,000 that the directors of George consider doubtful.

3.4 The interest-bearing borrowing of Bungle is repayable at par on 30 June 2006. Interest at 10% per annum is payable annually in arrears and the payment due on 30 June 2003 has already been made. The relevant discount rate is 7%.

3.5 The other provisions of Bungle comprise:

- $400,000 in respect of the closure of various retail outlets to which the directors of Bungle became committed prior to entering into acquisition negotiations with the directors of George.
- $800,000 in respect of the estimated cost of integrating Bungle into the George group. No detailed integration plans had been formulated by 30 June 2003.

3.6 The additional deferred tax that needs to be provided on the adjustments that are necessary as a result of the fair value exercise is a liability of $3 million.

4 George supplies a component to Zippy at cost plus a mark up of 20%. At 30 June 2003, the inventories of Zippy included $1·5 million in respect of this component. At 30 June 2003, the receivables of George showed an amount receivable from Zippy of $1·2 million, while the trade payables of Zippy showed an amount payable to George of $600,000. On 29 June 2003, George sent a consignment of components to Zippy at an invoiced price of $600,000. The consignment was received and recorded by Zippy on 2 July 2003.

5 On 15 July 2003, Zippy paid its preferred share dividend for the year ended 30 June 2003. George made no entries in its financial statements in respect of this dividend until it was received in cash.

6 Goodwill on consolidation is amortised over its estimated useful economic life of 20 years. The amortisation of goodwill on consolidation of Bungle commences on 1 July 2003.

6.1 In preparing its consolidated financial statements, George measures the assets and liabilities of subsidiaries using the allowed alternative treatment laid down in IAS 22.

Required:

(a) Compute the goodwill on consolidation of Bungle that will be shown in the consolidated balance sheet of George at 30 June 2003. Provide justification for your figures where you consider this is needed.

(14 marks)

(b) Prepare the consolidated balance sheet of George at 30 June 2003.

(16 marks)

(Total = 30 marks)

SECTION C – 50 MARKS

ANSWER TWO QUESTIONS ONLY

Question Three

You are the accountant of Acquirer. Your enterprise has the strategy of growth by acquisition and your directors have identified an enterprise, Target, which they wish to investigate with a view to launching a takeover bid. Your directors consider that the directors of Target will contest any bid and will not be very co-operative in providing background information on the enterprise. Therefore, relevant financial information is likely to be restricted to the publicly available financial statements.

Your directors have asked you to compute key financial ratios from the latest financial statements of Target [for the year ended 30 November 2002] and compare the ratios with those for other enterprises in a similar sector. Accordingly, you have selected ten broadly similar enterprises and have presented the directors with the following calculations:

Ratio	*Basis of calculation*	*Ratio for Target*	*Spread of ratios for comparative enterprises*		
			Highest	*Average*	*Lowest*
Gross profit margin	$\frac{\text{Gross profit}}{\text{Revenue}}$	42%	44%	38%	33%
Operating profit margin	$\frac{\text{Profit from operations}}{\text{Revenue}}$	29%	37%	30%	26%
Return on total capital	$\frac{\text{Profit from operations}}{\text{Total capital}}$	73%	92·5%	69%	52%
Interest cover	$\frac{\text{Profit from operations}}{\text{Finance cost}}$	1·8 times	3·2 times	2·5 times	1·6 times
Gearing	$\frac{\text{Debt capital}}{\text{Total capital}}$	52%	56%	40%	28%
Dividend cover	$\frac{\text{Profit after tax}}{\text{Dividend}}$	5·2 times	5 times	4 times	3 times
Turnover of inventory	$\frac{\text{Cost of sales}}{\text{Closing inventory}}$	4·4 times	4·5 times	4 times	3·2 times
Receivables days	$\frac{\text{Trade receivables}}{\text{1 day's sales revenue}}$	51 days	81 days	62 days	49 days

Required:

(a) Using the ratios provided, write a report that compares the financial performance and position of Target to the other enterprises in the survey. Where an issue arises that reflects particularly favourably or unfavourably on Target, you should assess its relevance to a potential acquirer.

(16 marks)

(b) Identify any reservations you have regarding the extent to which the ratios provided can contribute to an acquisition decision by the directors of Acquirer. You should highlight the extent to which the financial statements themselves might help you to overcome the reservations you have identified.

(9 marks)
(Total = 25 marks)

Question Four

You are the chief accountant of Ant, an enterprise that prepares financial statements in accordance with International Accounting Standards. Your assistant has prepared the first draft of the consolidated financial statements for the year ended 31 October 2003 and these show a profit after tax of $66 million, while the balance sheet shows ownership interests [total assets less total liabilities, including minority interests] of $450 million.

Your assistant has identified the following issues that require your review:

Issue (a)
An overseas subsidiary has made a loss (adjusted for tax purposes and appropriately translated into $s) of $15 million for the year ended 31 October 2003. Local tax legislation allows this loss to be relieved for tax purposes only against future profits of the same trade. Ant has no other subsidiaries in the same tax jurisdiction as this subsidiary. The loss is primarily due to a reduction in turnover caused by a reduction in demand for the product that the subsidiary produces. There is little indication that demand will be restored to its former levels in the foreseeable future.

Your assistant has recognised a deferred tax asset of $6 million in the draft financial statements, being the future tax consequences of the timing difference of $15 million, measured at the local tax rate of 40%. This deferred tax asset has been offset against deferred tax liabilities arising on timing differences originating in other tax jurisdictions.

Issue (b)
On 1 November 2002, Ant established a new subsidiary located in a jurisdiction where the unit of currency is the Franco. The initial investment was 40 million Francos (the initial net assets of the subsidiary). The investment was financed by a loan of 40 million Francos from a German bank. No capital repayments of the loan are due until 31 October 2022.

The exchange rate at 1 November 2002 was 1·6 Francos to $1. On 31 October 2003, the exchange rate was 1·5 Francos to $1. Due to large start-up costs, the subsidiary did not make a profit in the early months of trading and the net assets of the subsidiary at 31 October 2003 remained at 40 million Francos.

In preparing the draft consolidated financial statements, your assistant has translated both the loan and the financial statements of the subsidiary at 1·6 Francos to $1 on the basis that the financing of the subsidiary was obtained when the exchange rate was 1·6 Francos to $1. The subsidiary has its own distinct market presence and manufactures its products locally.

Issue (c)
On 1 November 2002, Ant issued two million $100 loan notes at $90 per note. A merchant bank received $4 million to underwrite the issue and Ant incurred other costs of $500,000 relating to the issue of the notes. The notes pay no interest and are redeemable at $135 per note on 31 October 2007. As an alternative to redemption, the notes can be converted into 50 equity shares per $100 note on 31 October 2007.

Your assistant has written off the issue costs of $4·5 million to the income statement for the year ended 31 October 2003 as an administrative expense and credited the proceeds of issue [$180 million] to a convertible loan notes account. He proposes to show this in the capital and reserves section of the balance sheet on the basis that the share price on 31 October 2007 is likely to be at least $4, so conversion, rather than repayment, is likely to be a near certainty.

Your assistant has been informed that, at 1 November 2002, the fair value of the options to convert the loan notes into shares on 31 October 2007 was $22·5 million. However, he does not consider this information to be relevant and so has ignored it.

Required:

For each of the three issues, evaluate the treatment adopted by your assistant with reference to currently published Accounting Standards. Where you consider the treatment adopted to be incorrect, you should state the journal adjustment required to correct the error.

In all cases, you should give any supporting explanations you consider appropriate to justify your conclusions.

The allocation of marks to the three issues is as follows:

Issue (a)	*(6 marks)*
Issue (b)	*(9 marks)*
Issue (c)	*(10 marks)*

(Total = 25 marks)

Question Five

You are the accountant responsible for training at Develop, an enterprise with a number of investments throughout the world. A key financial reporting task is to prepare consolidated financial statements and this forms an important aspect of the training of new accountants.

A recently-employed trainee has sent you this memorandum:

> I have just attended my first training course and have learned the mechanics of how to treat subsidiaries, associates, and trade investments in the consolidated accounts. I'm reasonably comfortable with the numbers but the concepts baffle me. Why does the exercise of adding together the balance sheets of our enterprise with those of our subsidiaries give our shareholders useful financial information? Why do we treat associates differently – I find the concept of adding together all the net assets and showing our share as one amount particularly confusing? I'm happier with the treatment of trade investments, at least I can see that the figure is what we paid to buy the shares. Why not do this for all our investments? I don't need a detailed explanation of the mechanics, which I'm already reasonably happy with.

Required:

(a) Draft a reply to your trainee that explains the principles underpinning the preparation of consolidated financial statements. You should clearly explain why subsidiaries, associates and trade investments are treated differently and why the information is of benefit to the shareholders of the investor.

(15 marks)

You also receive a memorandum from a slightly more experienced trainee:

> I've just attended my second training course and a couple of things confused me. First of all we were told that the net assets of newly-acquired subsidiaries need to be revalued to fair value at the date of acquisition. I don't see how this can produce sensible results unless the net assets of other group members are revalued at the same time. Then we were told about another method of consolidation, the uniting of interests method. This seemed a lot easier than the normal one. It seems that we don't need to worry about fair value adjustments under this method and we don't even have to distinguish between pre- and post-acquisition profits. What's more, it seems to produce higher reported profits! Why don't we use it all the time?

Required:

(b) Draft a reply to this second trainee that explains the rationale behind fair value adjustments and identifies the type of business combinations which might lead to the use of the uniting of interests method of consolidation. You do NOT need to explain the detailed mechanics of fair value adjustments or the uniting of interests method. However, you should refer to any relevant current developments.

(10 marks)

(Total = 25 marks)

Question Six

Global is an enterprise preparing financial statements in accordance with International Accounting Standards. Global has a subsidiary, Local, located in a jurisdiction that prepares financial statements in $ dollars in a format that is consistent with IAS 1 – *Presentation of Financial Statements* – but otherwise in accordance with local accounting standards

The financial statements of Local for the year ended 30 September 2003 [the group accounting date] are given below:

Income statement – year ended 30 September 2003:

	$000
Revenue	40,000
Cost of sales	(25,000)
Gross profit	15,000
Other operating expenses	(10,000)
Profit from operations	5,000
Profit on sale of land	2,000
Finance cost	(1,500)
Profit before tax	5,500
Income tax expense	(500)
Profit for the period	5,000

Balance sheet at 30 September 2003

	$000	*$000*
ASSETS		
Non-current assets:		
Property, plant and equipment	21,000	
Intangible assets	3,000	
		24,000
Current assets		7,000
		31,000
EQUITY AND LIABILITIES		
Capital and reserves:		
Issued capital	8,000	
Revaluation reserve	2,000	
Accumulated profits	8,000	
		18,000
Non-current liabilities		
Interest-bearing borrowings	9,000	
Deferred tax	1,000	
		10,000
Current liabilities		3,000
		31,000

The accountant of Local has informed you of the following transactions that have occurred during the year.

1 The directors of Local decided to make the balance sheet stronger by including their estimate of the value of key employees as an intangible non-current asset. They placed a value of $3 million on the asset and justified its inclusion on the basis that the expertise of key employees gave Local a clear competitive edge. No amortisation was charged on the basis that the asset was unlikely to lose value. The asset was incorporated into the financial statements by debiting non-current assets and crediting other operating expenses.

2 On 1 October 2002, Local sold a piece of land for $16 million, at a time when the carrying value of the land was $14 million and its market value $20 million. In preparing the financial statements for the year to 30 September 2003, Local recognised the revenue from the sale and eliminated the cost of the land, disclosing the profit on sale of $2 million separately in the income statement.

At the time of the sale, Local was given an option to repurchase the land on 30 September 2003, 2004 or 2005 on the following terms:

- 30 September 2003 $17·6 million
- 30 September 2004 $19·36 million
- 30 September 2005 $21·296 million

The option was not exercised on 30 September 2003 and is unlikely to be exercised on 30 September 2004 due to anticipated cash shortages in that year. However, the cash shortages are expected to be temporary and Local expects substantial accumulations of cash in 2005. The directors of Local expect the price of land to rise at around 12% per annum for the foreseeable future.

3 Local has a policy of periodically revaluing all its properties. All properties were revalued in the current period. One of the properties that was revalued during the year was a factory that had a carrying value prior to revaluation of $8 million. The current value of the property was estimated at $7 million. The deficit was caused by the fact that the product manufactured in the factory was no longer popular with customers. The deficit has been offset against the revaluation reserve on the basis that, although the factory had not previously been revalued, there was a balance of more than $1 million in the revaluation reserve relating to previous revaluations of other properties. Properties and land are regarded as separate classes of property, plant and equipment and land is not subject to periodic revaluations.

In other respects, the accounting practices followed by Local are in accordance with International Accounting Standards.

Required:

(a) Redraft the income statement and balance sheet of Local to reflect any adjustments that are necessary to ensure that they are prepared in accordance with International Accounting Standards. You should fully explain any adjustments you make by referring to necessary International Accounting Standards or frameworks.

Ignore any potential adjustments to deferred tax.

(20 marks)

(b) Discuss the suggestion that it would be easier for consolidation purposes if all group enterprises followed International Accounting Standards when preparing their individual financial statements.

(5 marks)

(Total = 25 marks)

End of paper

Maths Tables and Formulae are on the following pages

TABLES

Present value table

Present value of $1, that is $(1 + r)^{-n}$ where r = interest rate; n = number of periods until payment or receipt.

Periods	Interest rates (*r*)									
(*n*)	1%	2%	3%	4%	5%	6%	7%	8%	9%	10%
1	0.990	0.980	0.971	0.962	0.952	0.943	0.935	0.926	0.917	0.909
2	0.980	0.961	0.943	0.925	0.907	0.890	0.873	0.857	0.842	0.826
3	0.971	0.942	0.915	0.889	0.864	0.840	0.816	0.794	0.772	0.751
4	0.961	0.924	0.888	0.855	0.823	0.792	0.763	0.735	0.708	0.683
5	0.951	0.906	0.863	0.822	0.784	0.747	0.713	0.681	0.650	0.621
6	0.942	0.888	0.837	0.790	0.746	0705	0.666	0.630	0.596	0.564
7	0.933	0.871	0.813	0.760	0.711	0.665	0.623	0.583	0.547	0.513
8	0.923	0.853	0.789	0.731	0.677	0.627	0.582	0.540	0.502	0.467
9	0.914	0.837	0.766	0.703	0.645	0.592	0.544	0.500	0.460	0.424
10	0.905	0.820	0.744	0.676	0.614	0.558	0.508	0.463	0.422	0.386
11	0.896	0.804	0.722	0.650	0.585	0.527	0.475	0.429	0.388	0.350
12	0.887	0.788	0.701	0.625	0.557	0.497	0.444	0.397	0.356	0.319
13	0.879	0.773	0.681	0.601	0.530	0.469	0.415	0.368	0.326	0.290
14	0.870	0.758	0.661	0.577	0.505	0.442	0.388	0.340	0.299	0.263
15	0.861	0.743	0.642	0.555	0.481	0.417	0.362	0.315	0.275	0.239
16	0.853	0.728	0.623	0.534	0.458	0.394	0.339	0.292	0.252	0.218
17	0.844	0.714	0.605	0.513	0.436	0.371	0.317	0.270	0.231	0.198
18	0.836	0.700	0.587	0.494	0.416	0.350	0.296	0.250	0.212	0.180
19	0.828	0.686	0.570	0.475	0.396	0.331	0.277	0.232	0.194	0.164
20	0.820	0.673	0.554	0.456	0.377	0.312	0.258	0.215	0.178	0.149

Periods	Interest rates (*r*)									
(*n*)	11%	12%	13%	14%	15%	16%	17%	18%	19%	20%
1	0.901	0.893	0.885	0.877	0.870	0.862	0.855	0.847	0.840	0.833
2	0.812	0.797	0.783	0.769	0.756	0.743	0.731	0.718	0.706	0.694
3	0.731	0.712	0.693	0.675	0.658	0.641	0.624	0.609	0.593	0.579
4	0.659	0.636	0.613	0.592	0.572	0.552	0.534	0.516	0.499	0.482
5	0.593	0.567	0.543	0.519	0.497	0.476	0.456	0.437	0.419	0.402
6	0.535	0.507	0.480	0.456	0.432	0.410	0.390	0.370	0.352	0.335
7	0.482	0.452	0.425	0.400	0.376	0.354	0.333	0.314	0.296	0.279
8	0.434	0.404	0.376	0.351	0.327	0.305	0.285	0.266	0.249	0.233
9	0.391	0.361	0.333	0.308	0.284	0.263	0.243	0.225	0.209	0.194
10	0.352	0.322	0.295	0.270	0.247	0.227	0.208	0.191	0.176	0.162
11	0.317	0.287	0.261	0.237	0.215	0.195	0.178	0.162	0.148	0.135
12	0.286	0.257	0.231	0.208	0.187	0.168	0.152	0.137	0.124	0.112
13	0.258	0.229	0.204	0.182	0.163	0.145	0.130	0.116	0.104	0.093
14	0.232	0.205	0.181	0.160	0.141	0.125	0.111	0.099	0.088	0.078
15	0.209	0.183	0.160	0.140	0.123	0.108	0.095	0.084	0.079	0.065
16	0.188	0.163	0.141	0.123	0.107	0.093	0.081	0.071	0.062	0.054
17	0.170	0.146	0.125	0.108	0.093	0.080	0.069	0.060	0.052	0.045
18	0.153	0.130	0.111	0.095	0.081	0.069	0.059	0.051	0.044	0.038
19	0.138	0.116	0.098	0.083	0.070	0.060	0.051	0.043	0.037	0.031
20	0.124	0.104	0.087	0.073	0.061	0.051	0.043	0.037	0.031	0.026

Cumulative present value of $1 per annum, Receivable or Payable at the end of each year for *n* years

$$\frac{1-(1+r)^{-n}}{r}$$

Periods (*n*)	Interest rates (*r*) 1%	2%	3%	4%	5%	6%	7%	8%	9%	10%
1	0.990	0.980	0.971	0.962	0.952	0.943	0.935	0.926	0.917	0.909
2	1.970	1.942	1.913	1.886	1.859	1.833	1.808	1.783	1.759	1.736
3	2.941	2.884	2.829	2.775	2.723	2.673	2.624	2.577	2.531	2.487
4	3.902	3.808	3.717	3.630	3.546	3.465	3.387	3.312	3.240	3.170
5	4.853	4.713	4.580	4.452	4.329	4.212	4.100	3.993	3.890	3.791
6	5.795	5.601	5.417	5.242	5.076	4.917	4.767	4.623	4.486	4.355
7	6.728	6.472	6.230	6.002	5.786	5.582	5.389	5.206	5.033	4.868
8	7.652	7.325	7.020	6.733	6.463	6.210	5.971	5.747	5.535	5.335
9	8.566	8.162	7.786	7.435	7.108	6.802	6.515	6.247	5.995	5.759
10	9.471	8.983	8.530	8.111	7.722	7.360	7.024	6.710	6.418	6.145
11	10.368	9.787	9.253	8.760	8.306	7.887	7.499	7.139	6.805	6.495
12	11.255	10.575	9.954	9.385	8.863	8.384	7.943	7.536	7.161	6.814
13	12.134	11.348	10.635	9.986	9.394	8.853	8.358	7.904	7.487	7.103
14	13.004	12.106	11.296	10.563	9.899	9.295	8.745	8.244	7.786	7.367
15	13.865	12.849	11.938	11.118	10.380	9.712	9.108	8.559	8.061	7.606
16	14.718	13.578	12.561	11.652	10.838	10.106	9.447	8.851	8.313	7.824
17	15.562	14.292	13.166	12.166	11.274	10.477	9.763	9.122	8.544	8.022
18	16.398	14.992	13.754	12.659	11.690	10.828	10.059	9.372	8.756	8.201
19	17.226	15.679	14.324	13.134	12.085	11.158	10.336	9.604	8.950	8.365
20	18.046	16.351	14.878	13.590	12.462	11.470	10.594	9.818	9.129	8.514

Periods (*n*)	Interest rates (*r*) 11%	12%	13%	14%	15%	16%	17%	18%	19%	20%
1	0.901	0.893	0.885	0.877	0.870	0.862	0.855	0.847	0.840	0.833
2	1.713	1.690	1.668	1.647	1.626	1.605	1.585	1.566	1.547	1.528
3	2.444	2.402	2.361	2.322	2.283	2.246	2.210	2.174	2.140	2.106
4	3.102	3.037	2.974	2.914	2.855	2.798	2.743	2.690	2.639	2.589
5	3.696	3.605	3.517	3.433	3.352	3.274	3.199	3.127	3.058	2.991
6	4.231	4.111	3.998	3.889	3.784	3.685	3.589	3.498	3.410	3.326
7	4.712	4.564	4.423	4.288	4.160	4.039	3.922	3.812	3.706	3.605
8	5.146	4.968	4.799	4.639	4.487	4.344	4.207	4.078	3.954	3.837
9	5.537	5.328	5.132	4.946	4.772	4.607	4.451	4.303	4.163	4.031
10	5.889	5.650	5.426	5.216	5.019	4.833	4.659	4.494	4.339	4.192
11	6.207	5.938	5.687	5.453	5.234	5.029	4.836	4.656	4.486	4.327
12	6.492	6.194	5.918	5.660	5.421	5.197	4.988	7.793	4.611	4.439
13	6.750	6.424	6.122	5.842	5.583	5.342	5.118	4.910	4.715	4.533
14	6.982	6.628	6.302	6.002	5.724	5.468	5.229	5.008	4.802	4.611
15	7.191	6.811	6.462	6.142	5.847	5.575	5.324	5.092	4.876	4.675
16	7.379	6.974	6.604	6.265	5.954	5.668	5.405	5.162	4.938	4.730
17	7.549	7.120	6.729	6.373	6.047	5.749	5.475	5.222	4.990	4.775
18	7.702	7.250	6.840	6.467	6.128	5.818	5.534	5.273	5.033	4.812
19	7.839	7.366	6.938	6.550	6.198	5.877	5.584	5.316	5.070	4.843
20	7.963	7.469	7.025	6.623	6.259	5.929	5.628	5.353	5.101	4.870

FORMULAE

Annuity

Present value of an annuity of $1 per annum, receivable or payable for *n* years, commencing in one year, discounted at *r*% per annum:

$$PV = \frac{1}{r}\left[1 - \frac{1}{[1+r]^n}\right]$$

Perpetuity

Present value of $1 per annum, payable or receivable in perpetuity, commencing in one year, discounted at *r*% per annum:

$$PV = \frac{1}{r}$$

Growing perpetuity

Present value of $1 per annum, receivable or payable, commencing in one year, growing in perpetuity at a constant rate of *g*% per annum, discounted at *r*% per annum:

$$PV = \frac{1}{r - g}$$

The Examiner for IFRI offers to future candidates and to lecturers using this booklet for study purposes, the following background and guidance on the questions included in this examination paper.

Section A – compulsory

Question one provides a selection of 10 multiple-choice sub-questions, designed to cover the whole of the IFRI syllabus and to test candidates' knowledge, understanding and application.

Section B — compulsory

Question two: The preparation of consolidated financial statements will always be a key component of this question. The question tests the following learning outcomes:

- *prepare a consolidated balance sheet for a group of enterprises.*
- *explain and apply the concept of fair value at the point of acquisition.*

Section C — two questions from four

Question three requires candidates to analyse financial performance with reference to given accounting ratios and reflect on the limitations of ratio analysis as a means of performance measurement. The question tests the following learning outcomes:

- *evaluate financial statements and prepare a concise report on the results of the analysis.*
- *identify the limitations of analysis based on financial statements.*
- *explain the weaknesses of the financial report which reduce its effectiveness in communicating meaningful information to users.*

Question four tests candidates' ability to identify the appropriate accounting treatment for three complex transactions. The question tests the following learning outcomes:

- *explain and apply foreign currency translation principles.*
- *explain the difference between the closing rate/net investment method and the temporal method.*
- *explain the correct treatment for foreign loans financing foreign equity investments.*
- *explain the principles of profit measurement and alternative approaches to asset valuations.*
- *explain the difference between liabilities and shareholders' funds and allocate finance costs appropriately.*

Question five: Students have spent a considerable part of their study time for this subject on consolidated accounts. There will usually be a "specialised" consolidation question in section C to supplement the compulsory question that will always be in section B. The question tests the following learning outcomes:

- *explain the conditions required for an undertaking to be a subsidiary or an associate of a group.*
- *explain the concept of fair value at the point of acquisition.*
- *explain the concept of an associate and a joint venture.*
- *explain the uniting of interests method of consolidation.*
- *discuss emerging developments in financial reporting evidenced by discussion and exposure drafts issued by regulatory bodies.*

Question six focuses on the adjustment of financial statements to a common base for consolidation purposes and the benefits for group enterprises of using uniform accounting practices across the group. Knowledge of both of these issues is important for chartered management accountants at this level. The question tests the following learning outcomes:

- *explain the process of measuring, recording and disclosing the effect of exchanges between a business and its sociological environment – human resource accounting.*
- *explain the problems of profit measurement and alternative approaches to asset valuations.*
- *discuss the principles of substance over form to range of transactions.*
- *identify major differences between UK GAAP, IASs and US GAAP.*
- *Discuss emerging developments in financial reporting evidenced by discussion and exposure drafts issued by Regulatory bodies.*

The Examiner's Answers for Financial Reporting – International Accounting Standards

SECTION A

Answers to Question One

1.1	**A**	**B**	**Ⓒ**	**D**
1.2	**A**	**Ⓑ**	**C**	**D**
1.3	**A**	**B**	**C**	**Ⓓ**
1.4	**Ⓐ**	**B**	**C**	**D**
1.5	**A**	**Ⓑ**	**C**	**D**
1.6	**A**	**B**	**C**	**Ⓓ**
1.7	**A**	**B**	**Ⓒ**	**D**
1.8	**A**	**B**	**Ⓒ**	**D**
1.9	**Ⓐ**	**B**	**C**	**D**
1.10	**A**	**Ⓑ**	**C**	**D**

Answers to Objective Test Questions requiring calculations

1.1

In order to make the current assets of Parent consistent with the current liabilities of Child, the intra-group dividend receivable of $64,000 [80% x $80,000] needs to be included. This makes the current assets of Parent $664,000 and the net current assets of the group $464,000.

Therefore the correct answer is C

1.2

The minority interest is as follows:

	Ordinary	*Preferred*	*Total*
	$000	*$000*	*$000*
Total share capital	250	150	400
Total reserves	170	Nil	170
Total net assets	420	150	570
Minority interest (40%/60%)	168	90	258

Therefore the correct answer is B

1.4

The gain on sale is computed as follows:

	$	*$*
Disposal proceeds		4,000,000
Net assets relating to the disposal:		
• At 1 July 2002	8,500,000	
• $^{6}/_{12}$ x profit for the year to 30 June 2003	400,000	
• At 31 December 2002	8,900,000	
• 35% relates to the disposal		(3,115,000)
Goodwill relating to the disposal:		
• Total as given	1,000,000	
• $^{138}/_{240}$ unamortised at 31 December 2002	575,000	
• $^{35}/_{75}$ relates to the disposal		(268,333)
Gain on sale		616,667

Therefore the correct answer is A

1.5

The computation is as follows:

	$	$
Opening net assets [40 million florins]:		
• At opening rate (2·5)	16,000,000	
• At closing rate (2·0)	20,000,000	
• Gain on opening net assets		4,000,000
Profit for the year [4·5 million florins]		
• At average rate (2·25)	2,000,000	
• At closing rate (2·0)	2,250,000	
• Gain on profit		250,000
Overall gain on retranslation		4,250,000
Group share (80%)		3,400,000

Therefore the correct answer is B

1.6

The overall impairment loss is $2 million [$27 million - $25 million]. This loss is first allocated to the asset that has suffered obvious impairment, leaving the balance of $1 million to be allocated to goodwill.

Therefore the correct answer is D

1.7

Under the provisions of IAS 12, deferred tax is provided on the revaluation surplus since it creates a temporary difference. The deferred tax implications of the loss can be recognised if the loss is due to non-recurring factors, and taxable profits are expected in the future. Therefore the corrected deferred tax liability is $8 million + 30% x $7 million - 30% x $2 million = $9·5 million.

Therefore the correct answer is C

1.8

The finance cost is composed of three elements:

- The **direct** costs of issue ($500,000).
- The interest payable ($50 million x 4% x 5 = $10 million).
- The premium payable on repayment of $10 million.

Therefore the correct answer is C

1.9

Statements (i) and (ii) are both true. The net pension asset is the market value of the assets of the scheme [which decreases when share prices fall], less the present value of the scheme liabilities [which decreases when interest rates rise]. Statement (iii) is false. Variations to benefits that relate to past service should be recognised immediately if they vest immediately.

Therefore the correct answer is A

1.10

The initial amount provided is $2,268,000 [$4,000,000 x 0·567]. This is the present value of $4 million payable in 5 years at a cost of capital of 12%. The debit is to non-current assets since the expenditure gives access to future economic benefits. Therefore, the total charge to income for the year to 30 June 2003 is:

- Depreciation – 20% x $2,268,000 = $453,600.
- Unwinding of discount – 12% x $2,268,000 = $272,160.
- Total $725,760.

Therefore the correct answer is B

SECTION B

Answer to Question Two

Requirement (a)

Step 1 – fair value of net assets acquired

Description	*Fair value $000*	*Comment*
Land and buildings	18,000	Market value
Plant and machinery	13,750	Depreciated replacement cost [$^5/_8$ x $22 million]
Inventory	11,600	Selling price less profit allowance [$11·5 million] + scrap value [$100,000]
Receivables	8,600	Reduced by provision for doubtful receivable
Current liabilities	(10,000)	Book value
Long term loan	(4,314)	Present value of future cash flows [see working]
Deferred tax	(4,500)	Book value plus $3 million
Other provisions	(400)	$800,000 a post-acquisition item
	32,736	

Step 2 – fair value of consideration given (in $000)
- Shares – 8,000 x ¾ x $4 = $24,000
- Deferred cash – 8,000 x 0·873 = $6,984
- Total $30,984

Step 3 – compute goodwill (in $000)
$30,984 – 80% x $32,736 = $4,795.

Working – present value of loan repayments using a 7% discount rate (in $000):

400 x 2·624 + 4,000 x 0·816 = $4,314.

Requirement (b)

Consolidated balance sheet of George at 30 June 2003

	$000	*$000*
Assets		
Non-current assets:		
Property, plant and equipment [45,000 + 25,000 + 18,000 + 13,750]	101,750	
Goodwill (requirement a)	4,795	
		106,545
Current assets:		
Inventories [18,000 + 12,000 + 11,600 - 250 (working 1)	41,350	
Inventory in transit [600 - 100 (working 1)]	500	
Receivables [15,000 + 10,000 + 8,600 - 1,200]	32,400	
		74,250
Total assets		180,795

	$000	$000
Equity and liabilities		
Capital and reserves:		
Ordinary share capital [25,000 + 6,000]		31,000
Share premium account [10,000 + 6,000 x $3]		28,000
Accumulated profits [working 3]		32,150
		91,150
Minority interest [working 2]		11,547
Non-current liabilities		
Long term loan [20,000 + 4,314]	24,314	
Deferred consideration	6,984	
Deferred tax [2,000 + 4,500 + 1,000]	7,500	
Other	400	
		39,198
Current liabilities		
Trade payables [10,000 + 6,500 + 6,000 - 600]	21,900	
Tax payable [2,000 + 1,000 + 1,500]	4,500	
Other payables [1,000 - 500]	500	
Bank overdraft [5,000 + 4,000 + 3,000]	12,000	
		38,900
Total equity and liabilities		180,795

Working 1 – unrealised profit [in $000s]:

- On inventory in hand [1,500 x $\frac{20}{120}$] = $250
- On inventory in transit [600 x $\frac{20}{120}$] = $100

Working 2 – minority interest

	$000
In Zippy – 50% x $10 million	5,000
In Bungle – 20% x $32·736 million – see requirement (a)	6,547
	11,547

Working 3 – accumulated profits

	$000
George	24,000
Dividend receivable from Zippy	500
Zippy	8,000
Unrealised profit [250 + 100 – see working 1]	(350)
	32,150

SECTION C

Answer to Question Three

Requirement (a)

Report on the ratios and their implications

To: The board of directors of Acquirer

From: Accountant

Subject: Proposed acquisition of Target

Date: 19 November 2003

Following our earlier discussions, I have computed key ratios for Target and some similar enterprises. These are attached as an appendix to this report.

It is notable that the gross profit margin of Target is towards the upper end of the range of comparison, while the net margin is towards the lower end. The relatively high gross margin could be due to a sales mix of relatively more profitable products or, alternatively, because of a tighter than average control of costs. Given apparent problems in controlling other operating expenses (see below) a different sales mix is perhaps the most likely explanation.

The superior performance at gross margin level is largely negated by an apparently extremely poor control of other operating expenses. These seem to be running at around 13% of revenue as against 7 or 8% for the enterprises in the sample. It may be that the costs are being incurred to finance future growth and cannot be capitalised under existing accounting standards. However, they could equally be due to inherent inefficiencies and this issue will certainly require further investigation before proceeding further.

Return on capital is slightly higher than the average for the sample and given that net profit margin is towards the lower end, this implies a ratio of revenue to capital that is towards the upper end of the range revealed by the sample. This is quite encouraging as capital investment does appear to produce strong revenue streams provide costs can be controlled.

Interest cover is towards the lower end of the range of comparison and gearing is towards the upper end. There is a good chance these two issues are linked as other things being equal you would expect interest cover to vary in inverse proportion to gearing. The level of gearing may not be a key factor in an acquisition decision as we may well wish to refinance the enterprise if it becomes a subsidiary.

Dividend cover is relatively high compared with other enterprises in the sample. This could be due to a strategic decision by current management to retain a greater proportion of profits, but it could equally well be indicative of a strain on liquidity and this issue would require further investigation. However, the level of past dividend payout will not necessarily be a key future issue since, if Target becomes our subsidiary, we will be in a position to determine dividend levels within legal constraints.

Both inventory turnover and receivables days are towards the higher end of the performance range. This is a good sign which might have been expected given the relatively high turnover of capital that Target seems to enjoy.

I hope you find this report useful. Please do not hesitate to contact me if you have any queries regarding its contents.

Yours sincerely

Accountant

Requirement (b)

Limitations of the ratios

One key factor is the appropriateness of the sample as a basis for comparison with Target. It is inevitably subjective to identify 10 enterprises that are valid for this purpose. It is rare to find two enterprises with exactly the same operating environments and there may well have been a number of other equally valid samples of 10 enterprises that would have produced different ratios and therefore a different interpretation.

Another issue is the extent to which conventional ratios are computed from the results of a single accounting period. Different enterprises have different year ends and in the case of Target the most recently available financial statements are nearly a year old. The latest available financial statements could be for a period that is not typical of the trend of performance over a longer period due to unusual or non-recurring items. There is also the inherent problem of computing a ratio such as return on capital, where a performance figure, like profit, is expressed as a ratio or percentage of a position figure like capital.

A further key factor to bear in mind is that, despite the existence of an increasingly complex regulatory framework, enterprises still have considerable discretion in the manner that the financial statements are prepared and presented given the significant amount of judgement that is involved in selecting accounting policies.

A final factor to bear in mind is that financial ratios inevitably focus on historical financial aspects. Many useful performance indicators are non-financial in nature. It is possible to compute non-financial ratios, but these are often difficult to compare between enterprises given the voluntary nature of much non-financial information that is currently disclosed. It is also questionable as to how much historical financial data can contribute to a future acquisition decision.

The financial statements themselves would be of some assistance in overcoming the defects mentioned in the report above. They would provide information on the key accounting policies followed by the enterprise and would provide separate disclosure of non-recurring items. They may well also provide a degree of non-financial information and some predictions about the future prospects of the enterprise. However, as stated earlier, this information is unlikely to be as highly regulated as the historical financial data and so its reliability may be questioned.

Answer to Question Four

Issue (a)

The tax loss is a temporary difference, because the transactions giving rise to the tax loss have already been included in the financial statements and these transactions have potential future tax consequences, in that tax relief will be available if the subsidiary makes future profits. Economic benefits will potentially flow to the group as a result of this transaction, so the potential deferred tax implications are to create a deferred tax asset. IAS 12 – *Deferred tax* – states that, in theory, deferred tax assets can be recognised in exactly the same way as deferred tax liabilities. However, the usual recoverability test for assets needs to be applied. IAS 12 states that before a deferred tax asset can be recognised it must be more likely than not that there will be suitable taxable profits which can absorb the deductible temporary difference. In the scenario mentioned in issue (a), it is clear that we do not have this assurance and so recognition of a deferred tax asset would be inappropriate. In these circumstances, the deferred tax asset should be derecognised and the following journal entry is needed:

DEBIT: Tax charge in the income statement.
CREDIT: Non-current liabilities.
With $6,000,000.

Issue (b)

The loan is a monetary liability in the balance sheet of Ant and IAS 21 – *The Effects of changes in foreign exchange rates* – requires that monetary items be translated at the rate of exchange in force at the balance sheet date. This would mean restating the loan from its original carrying value of $25 million [40 million Francos/1·6] to $26,666,667 [[40 million Francos/1·5]. The resulting exchange loss of $1,666,667 would be reported in the income statement as a financing item.

The net assets of the subsidiary would be translated using the rate of exchange in force at the balance sheet date because the subsidiary is relatively independent of the parent on a day-to-day basis. Because the net assets of the subsidiary are the same as the loan balance, its closing $ value would also be $26,666,667. There would be an exchange gain of $1,666,667 on the retranslation of the opening net assets which IAS 21 would require is taken to equity.

Where a foreign currency loan is used to finance a foreign currency equity investment then IAS 21 requires a form of hedge accounting to be used in the consolidated financial statements [as well as in the financial statements of the parent]. Exchange differences arising on a monetary item that, in substance, forms part of the net investment in a foreign entity should be classified as equity until the disposal of the net investments. At that time they should be released to income along with the cumulative exchange differences on the relevant net investments.

The correcting journal entry will be:

DEBIT: Net assets
CREDIT: Long term loans.
With $1,666,667. No net exchange differences will be reported because the exchange differences on the loan and the net investment are both taken to equity and they are equal and opposite.

Issue (c)

The loan is a compound financial instrument and IAS 32 – *Financial instruments: Disclosure and Presentation* – requires that such instruments be classified in two component parts in the balance sheet of the issuer. This requirement is unaffected by the likelihood or otherwise that the holders of the instrument will exercise their conversion options. In this case, we are provided with the fair value of the option element [which does not change over the period] so the loan element can be derived by deducting the option element from the total initial carrying value of the instrument.

IAS 39 – *Financial instruments: Recognition and Measurement* requires that financial liabilities should be initially measured at "cost". Cost is the proceeds received minus the issue costs. Therefore, in this case "cost" is $175·5 million [$180 million - $4·5 million]. The loan element of the instrument is $153 million [$175·5 million - $22·5 million]. Since the loan is a held to maturity financial liability it should subsequently be re-measured at amortised cost using the effective interest method to measure the annual finance cost. The finance cost should be a constant percentage of the outstanding loan for each period.

In this case, the percentage can be found from tables:

- The initial loan amount is $153 million [A].
- The terminal loan amount with no interim payments is $270 million [B].
- A/B is 0·567.
- From tables this equates to an annual interest rate of 12%.

Therefore, the finance cost for the first year is $18,360,000 [$153 million x 12%] and the closing loan is $171,360,000. The correcting journal entry that is required is:

	DR	*CR*
	$000	*$000*
Shareholders funds – initial entry	180,000	
Shareholders funds – option element		22,500
Long term loans		171,360
Income statement – admin expenses		4,500
Income statement – finance cost	18,360	

Answer to Question Five

Requirement (a)

Consolidated financial statements show the resources deployed by a single economic entity and the return generated by those resources. The boundary of the single economic entity is determined by common control. Control is essentially the ability to direct the operating and financial policies of an entity. IAS 27 – *Consolidated financial statements and accounting for investments in subsidiaries* – defines a subsidiary in terms of the ability of the parent to exercise control. This is why a group consists of a parent undertaking and its subsidiary undertakings. Because this single economic entity [comprising more than one separate legal entities] is under common control, it is logical to show one balance sheet containing 100% of the controlled resources and one income statement containing 100% of the returns earned by those resources. However, a further function of financial statements is to show the interests of the investors in the resources under common control, so the ownership interests section of the balance sheet needs to separately identify the interests of the parent undertaking's shareholders from those of other "minority" investors in the economic entity.

It is inappropriate to treat associates and trade investments the way we treat subsidiaries because they are outside the boundary of control. However, associates do qualify for special treatment. Although the parent undertaking cannot control the deployment of resources, it is in a position to exercise a significant degree of influence over their deployment. If they actively exercise this significant influence, then mere inclusion of the initial amount invested, plus the amounts that happen to be received as dividends, is unlikely to adequately reflect the extent of the investor's interest. Therefore, although full consolidation is inappropriate, because control is not present, a special form of treatment is needed. This treatment, known as the equity method of consolidation, shows the investor's share of the net assets of the associate and its share of its profits.

Trade investments do not qualify for special treatment because control or significant influence is not present. If there is no control or influence over resources, then it is inappropriate to show those resources in any way in the consolidated balance sheet and it is better to show the initial amount invested. Similarly, if there is not control or influence over the distribution of profits then it is better to restrict amounts included in the consolidated income statement to dividends received.

Requirement (b)

The rationale behind fair value adjustments is essentially that when a new subsidiary joins a group that group has made an acquisition. It is effectively the case that the group has purchased the net assets of the newly acquired subsidiary. Therefore, the principle of fair value that is laid out in IAS 22 – *Business combinations* – is that it represents the amount that would be exchanged for each individual asset or liability in an arms length transaction between independent parties. It is essentially an application of the historical concept and adjustments are only made for the acquired subsidiary because only the acquired subsidiary has joined the group at a particular date.

The vast majority of business combinations involve the effective acquisition of a subsidiary by an existing group. However, IAS 22 identifies a category of business combinations that essentially involves the pooling of existing, separate, ownership interests to form a larger group. In such circumstances, neither sets of existing owners can be regarded as the dominant party and therefore it is misleading to talk about an acquiring and an acquired entity. This is the context in which the uniting of interests method of consolidation (sometimes known as the pooling of interests method) may well be appropriate. This means that (as stated at the start of this paragraph) merger accounting is only appropriate in a relatively restricted set of circumstances.

Where uniting of interests accounting is appropriate, the consolidation procedures are somewhat different. It would not be sensible to make fair value adjustments for part only of the newly formed group, because no "acquisition" is perceived to have taken place. Similarly, the concept of "pre-acquisition profits" has no place in the application of the uniting of interests method of consolidation. However, the circumstances in which the uniting of interests method is appropriate are somewhat unclear and a growing body of opinion internationally seems to suggest that a single method of consolidation, the acquisition (or "purchase") method should be used when preparing consolidated financial statements. The International Accounting Standards Board has indicated that it proposes to ban the use of uniting of interests accounting.

Answer to Question Six

Requirement (a)

Income statement – year ended 30 September 2003:

	$000
Revenue	40,000
Cost of sales	(25,000)
Gross profit	15,000
Other operating expenses (10,000 + 3,000 {W1})	(13,000)
Profit from operations	2,000
Impairment of property (W3)	(1,000)
Finance cost (1,500 + 1,600 {W2})	(3,100)
Loss before tax	(2,100)
Tax	(500)
Loss for the year after tax	(2,600)

Balance sheet at 30 September 2003

	$000	*$000*
Assets		
Non-current assets:		
Property, plant and equipment (21,000 + 14,000 {W2})	35,000	
Intangible assets (W1)	Nil	
		35,000
Current assets		7,000
		42,000
Equity and liabilities		
Capital and reserves:		
Issued capital	8,000	
Revaluation reserve (W4)	3,000	
Accumulated profits (W5)	400	
		11,400
Non-current liabilities		
Long term loans (9,000 + 17,600 {W2})	26,600	
Deferred tax	1,000	
		27,600
Current liabilities		3,000
		42,000

Workings

1. Intangible asset

IAS 38 only allows recognition of internally developed intangible assets if they have a readily ascertainable market value. This means that they must belong to a homogeneous population and there must exist an active market in the type of intangible asset that is being recognised. This is clearly not the case with employee expertise and so recognition is inappropriate. Therefore the $3 million debit to intangible assets and the credit to other operating expenses should be reversed.

2. "Sale" of land

Recognition of revenue on the "sale" of land seems inappropriate. IAS 18 – *Revenue* – requires that (inter-alia) the following conditions need to be satisfied before revenue from the sale of goods can be recognised:

- The enterprise has transferred to the buyer the significant risks and rewards of ownership of the goods.
- The enterprise retains neither continuing managerial involvement to the degree usually associated with ownership nor effective control over the goods sold.

Neither of the above conditions has been satisfied and so recognition of revenue seems inappropriate. It is clear that the option to "repurchase" is highly likely to be exercised in September 2005 and so a valid "sale" has never taken place. Therefore, the "sale" should be reversed. The IASC Framework for the preparation and presentation of financial statements states that reliable financial information should account for transactions according to their economic reality rather than their legal form. The "sales proceeds" of $16 million effectively represent a financial liability. It seems from the repurchase prices that are quoted that the effective interest rate on the loan is 10% per annum.

The following adjustments are necessary:

	DR	*CR*	
	$000	*$000*	
Non-current assets	14,000		The original carrying value
Profit on "sale"	2,000		
Finance cost	1,600		10% x $16 million
Long term loan		17,600	The expected repayment date is 30/9/2005

3. Revaluation deficit on property

The deficit is caused by a consumption of economic benefits and so under IAS 36 – *Impairment of assets* – is regarded as an impairment. IAS 36 states that impairment losses relating to revalued assets should be regarded as revaluation deficits and accounted for in accordance with IAS 16 – *Property, plant and equipment*. Revaluation deficits are taken to the income statements unless the revaluation reserve contains an equivalent amount in respect of a previous revaluation of the same asset. Therefore, this deficit should be recognised in the income statement. In view of the amount involved, it could arguably be separately disclosed as an exceptional item.

4. Closing balance revaluation reserve

	$000
Balance as stated	2,000
Transfer reversed from accumulated profits (W3)	1,000
Closing balance	3,000

5. Closing balance on accumulated profits

	$000
Opening balance ($8 million - $5 million)	3,000
Loss for the year	(2,600)
Closing balance	400

Requirement (b)

The use of International Accounting Standards by all group enterprises would certainly make consolidation more straightforward. Where group enterprises use different accounting standards, then adjustments need to be made to individual financial statements so as to ensure that the consolidation is based on financial statements that are prepared under the same accounting policies. The time and expense of this exercise would be avoided if all enterprises used the same accounting policies.

However, group enterprises are usually required to file their individual financial statements in their own jurisdiction. Unless local regulations allow filing using International Accounting Standards, the use of International Accounting Standards across the group is unlikely to be practicable. However, jurisdictions across the world are increasingly accepting International Accounting Standards for local filing purposes and, in the medium term, the whole-scale adoption of such standards may well be perfectly practicable.

However, at present, certain jurisdictions (the USA in particular) are resistant to the use of international standards on the grounds that they represent a watered down version of their own standards. Even so, the IASB is strongly committed to the enhancement of their programme and recent accounting scandals in the USA may lead to US standard setters being more prepared to adopt a more international agenda.

ELSEVIER

CIMA PUBLISHING

Order Form

for 4th Edition CIMA Official *Study Systems* (for 2004 Exams)

Qty	Abbrev	Title	ISBN	Price	Total
	FAFN	Financial Accounting Fundamentals	0750661046	£33.00	
	FMAF	Management Accounting Fundamentals	0750661054	£33.00	
	FECB	Economics for Business	0750661062	£33.00	
	FBLW	Business Law	0750661070	£33.00	
	FBSM	Business Mathematics	0750661089	£33.00	
	IFIN	Finance	0750661097	£33.00	
	IBTX	Business Taxation	0750661100	£33.00	
	IFNA	Financial Accounting UK Standards	0750661119	£33.00	
	IFAI	Financial Accounting International Standards	0750661127	£33.00	
	IFRP	Financial Reporting UK Standards	0750661135	£33.00	
	IFRI	Financial Reporting International Standards	0750661143	£33.00	
	IMPM	Management Accounting Performance Management	0750661151	£33.00	
	IDEC	Management Accounting Decision Making	075066116X	£33.00	
	ISPM	Systems and Project Management	0750661178	£33.00	
	IORG	Organisational Management	0750661186	£33.00	
	FLBS	Business Strategy	0750661194	£33.00	
	FLFS	Financial Strategy	0750661208	£33.00	
	FLIS	Information Strategy	0750661216	£33.00	
	FLCS	Case Study	0750661224	£33.00	
		Postage & packing		£2.95	
		TOTAL			

Cheques payable to Elsevier

CIMA Publishing is an imprint of Elsevier

Registered Office: The Boulevard, Langford Lane, Kidlington, Oxford OX5 1GB, UK

Registered in England: 3099304, VAT 494 627212

Elsevier retains certain personal information about you in hard copy form and on computer. It will be used to inform you about goods and services from Elsevier and its associated companies in which you may be interested. ☐ Please tick this box if you do not want to receive this information.

Post this form to:

CIMA Publishing Customer Services
Elsevier
FREEPOST (OF 1639)
Linacre House, Jordan Hill
OXFORD, OX2 8DP, UK

Or **FAX** (01865) 474 011
Or **PHONE** (01865) 474 014
Email: cimaorders@elsevier.com
www.cimapublishing.com

Name: ______________________

Organisation: ______________________

Invoice Address: ______________________

____

____

____

Postcode: ______________________

Phone number: ______________________

Email: ______________________

Delivery Address if different:

FAO ______________________

Address ______________________

____

____

____

Postcode ______________________

Please note that all deliveries must be signed for

Please charge my:

☐ Visa/Barclaycard ☐ Access/Mastercard

☐ American Express ☐ Diners Card

☐ Switch Issue No.

Card No. ______________________

Expiry Date ______________________

Cardholder Name: ______________________

Signature: ______________________

Date: ______________________

CPSIA information can be obtained at www.ICGtesting.com
Printed in the USA
LVOW032353150512

281913LV00012B/12/P

9 780750 662376